Military post library ass. of the United States

Life of Captain Nathan Hale

the martyr-spy of the revolution

Military post library ass. of the United States

Life of Captain Nathan Hale
the martyr-spy of the revolution

ISBN/EAN: 9783337092085

Printed in Europe, USA, Canada, Australia, Japan

Cover: Foto ©ninafisch / pixelio.de

More available books at **www.hansebooks.com**

LIFE

OF

CAPTAIN NATHAN HALE,

THE MARTYR-SPY OF THE REVOLUTION.

"EVERY KIND OF SERVICE NECESSARY FOR THE PUBLIC
GOOD BECOMES HONORABLE BY BEING NECESSARY."
"I ONLY REGRET THAT I HAVE BUT ONE LIFE TO LOSE FOR
MY COUNTRY."

NEW YORK:

U. S. Military Post Library Association.

1874.

NATHAN HALE.

THE business of the spy, though necessary in war, is one held in little honor, and the history is a brief one. If successful, nothing more is said; if he fail, and is detected, the penalty of death is at once inflicted, and the story is ended.

Doubtless, in our revolution, as in all wars, many spies were employed — but when, or where, or how has never been recorded. The one spy, who made a mark in our annals, was André, the Englishman; the man chosen to communicate with Arnold, the traitor. Many circumstances combined to invest his fate with interest, and to make even his enemies regret the necessity which, in time of war, leaves for the spy no sentence but death.

After Arnold had gone to New York, and taken his place in the British army, a man named Champe, with the connivance of some of his officers, pretended to desert,

(3)

served in the British lines, and faithfully
kept his place, waiting long for the opportunity to deliver up Arnold to the American
authorities. But by an accident, or a providence, on the very night when Champe
was to be on guard, when boats from our
side were ready to meet him, and his
plan seemed on the eve of accomplishment,
Arnold changed his quarters, and the whole
design fell through. With difficulty Champe
escaped, and returned to our lines. Had he
been taken, his fate had been sealed, as
a spy.

When the penalty of detection is certain
death, but two motives may induce a man
to embark in so hazardous an undertaking.
One is, the hope of large reward; the other,
genuine love of his country. One who, for
any reason, cares little for life, and cares
much for money, may be induced to run the
risk, and act as a spy. Or one who values
his life lightly, compared with the service
which he may be able to render; who is
willing to incur the danger of a terrible
death, if he may but serve the cause of
truth and freedom; one who has true patriotism, may consent to perform a service
combining great risks and little honor.

There are occasions in the conduct of the war when the obtaining of information is all-important, and when it can be gained in no other way but by visiting the enemy's camp, to learn, if possible, his present state and future plans.

Among those whom the history of our country should have made memorable, yet whose name is little known, and his story still less, stands NATHAN HALE, the spy. He died in the service of his country, — our country, — a noble martyr to a noble cause; and yet, if you speak of him, nine out of ten will ask, " Who was Nathan Hale? I never heard of him." And when we would study his character and history we find the materials most meager and unsatisfactory.

Before any attempt was made to honor his memory, much time had passed, and when the tardy justice of some of his countrymen would raise a monument to his memory, the records of his life were almost lost. He was sent by Washington, as a spy, into the British camp, was detected, condemned, and executed as a spy, and the place of his burial was never known.

A few more particulars we learn upon further inquiry.

HIS EARLY LIFE.

Nathan Hale was born in Coventry, Conn., on the 6th of June, 1755. Of a large family of twelve children, nine sons and three daughters, he was the sixth. His mother's maiden name was Elizabeth Strong; his father was Richard Hale, third in descent from John Hale, the first minister of Beverly, Mass. His father was an honest, upright, Christian man, and as farmer, magistrate, and deacon of the church, performed his duties, and maintained his position faithfully and honorably. His boys were trained in true New England habits, hardy, self-reliant, honest, and true. They assisted in the work of the farm, where every thing was done in its season, work promptly finished, the Sabbath observed as a day of rest; and, as most of the old Puritans of that time followed the Jewish custom of commencing the day at sunset, we may imagine the calm and quiet preparation of the Saturday evening, when, the labors of the day having been early finished, the rest and peace of the holy day began at the going down of the sun.

If this was not the town, it was very near

the one, where the first settlers, not having, in the midst of their early labors, time to frame a code of laws for themselves, voted to take the laws of God for their guidance, until such time as they could prepare something better.

Few traits or anecdotes of Hale's boyhood are preserved. The house in which he lived is still standing — a large, double, two-storied, old-fashioned house, with no attempt at ornament or fair proportions, but with plenty of room within and without, outhouses, and spreading orchards and shady trees. There Hale and his brothers pursued their work and their sports. He was not a strong child, but his vigorous training, simple food, and out-door exercise, strengthened his constitution, and imparted that energy and spirit which so well fitted him for the life he was to lead. He was fond of hunting and fishing, running, leaping, wrestling, and all athletic sports, the exercises that make *men* of muscle and vigor — *live men*.

After receiving such education as the village school afforded, Nathan, with two of his brothers, was placed under the care of Dr. Joseph Huntington, the minister of the parish. Schools of a higher order were not common in those days, and it was the custom for the minister to receive and educate such boys as wished to prepare for college. Happily for these boys, their teacher was a man of learning and acquirements, much respected for his talents, and a good and holy man.

COLLEGE LIFE.

In 1770, at the age of fifteen, Nathan Hale entered Yale College, at New Haven, where he pursued his course of study with diligence, faithfulness, and success. His tutors spoke well of him, and he made many friends, among all of whom he was distinguished for his high scholarship, his good principles, and his pleasant, cordial manners. He was particularly fond of mathematics and scientific pursuits, standing among the first of his class in these departments.

He did not make himself a mere bookworm, but continued his habits of vigorous exercise, and for a long time the marks of a tremendous leap which he once made upon the College Green were preserved; proving that, while cultivating his mind, he did not neglect to keep his body in good training.

ENGAGES IN TEACHING.

Hale graduated in September, 1773, among the first thirteen in a class of thirty-six, and on leaving college, as was the case with many young men in those days, entered on the discipline of teaching before commencing the study of his profession. He took a school, the first year, at East Haddam, in Connecticut, a quiet, secluded place, but possessing wealth and business activity. A lady who knew him there, thus spoke of him long afterward : " Every body loved him ; he was so sprightly, intelligent, kind, and withal *so handsome.*"

The next year he was invited to teach a larger school in New London. This was a select school, requiring in the teacher a good education and high attainments, while none could obtain the place but one whose character bore the "strictest scrutiny." There Hale taught acceptably and satisfactorily to himself and to the people. He had the care of over thirty boys in English and classical studies, during the day ; and in addition, a school for girls from *five to seven in the morning,* which hours he devoted to them.

All who knew him in New London spoke
in the same terms of his fair and irreproach-
able life ; his high moral character ; his fine
powers and attainments; his remarkable
success as a teacher, combining mildness
with decision, commanding at once respect
and affection.   Added to all, his pleasant
and most engaging manners seem to have
rendered him a general favorite among all
with whom he was brought in contact.

CHRISTIAN CHARACTER.

The   excellence of his character was
crowned by strong Christian principle. His
education had prepared him for a life of
usefulness.   The teachings of his father
conformed to the old Bible rule, — there
can be no better, — " Fear God, and keep
his commandments, for this is the whole
duty of man."   How early his resolution
was formed we are not told ; but the object
of his education from the beginning was to
prepare him, together with his two brothers, for the Christian ministry, and it was
considered a fit training for a minister of the
gospel to discipline himself and learn the
art of reaching the heart, and of imparting
knowledge, by teaching the young, and so

gaining experience and knowledge of human nature.

Hale possessed great ingenuity and diligence, and used to say laughingly to the young girls of his acquaintance, that he "could do every thing but spin." In his diary, kept for a short period, he writes, " A man never ought to lose a moment's time; if he puts off a thing from one minute to the next, his reluctance is but increased;" and he seems to have conformed his practice to this rule.

" In hight he was about five feet ten inches, and exceedingly well proportioned. His figure was fine and commanding. He had a broad, full chest, full face, light blue eyes, clear complexion, and hair of a medium brown. He had a light, elastic frame, and could put his hand upon a fence as high as his head and clear it at a bound. His face was full of intelligence and benevolence, of good sense and good feeling."

We have no diary of his remaining, no record of frames and feelings. The journal which he kept for a short time is a mere notice of events in his daily life; but thus much we may find: a scrupulous regard to truth and justice; self-denial and care for others; a habit of attending to religious duties, and upon religious services always on the Sabbath, when it was in his power. His only inquiry seems to have been, not, was a thing pleasant, agreeable, popular, polite, but, was it *right*. And the path of duty was the path he chose, without looking to see what the end should be, well knowing that the end must be, whatever the result, the approval of his own conscience, and of Him who gave and who rules the conscience.

THE SUMMONS TO ARMS.

April 19, 1775. Hale had been so engaged for two years, when the alarm at Lexington rang through the nation, arousing all to action, as one man. The news came from Boston to New London by express — not the lightning telegraph nor the swift railway car, but a man riding fast from one town to another spread the alarm, changing his horse when he was weary, and giving up his errand to another when he himself was too much worn out to go any further. So the news sped through the land. So slow was communication in those days, that in a small town in Connecticut, not thirty miles from the Sound, the news of the battle of Bunker Hill was only received three weeks after it had happened.

The news of Lexington reached New London, and the people were at once aroused. Public meetings were called, strong expressions of patriotism poured forth, and those who were ready set out at once. They had long and weary marches, through a country as yet but thinly settled, and with few means of transportation.

At the first meeting which was called the voice of Nathan Hale was heard. His soul was awake, and he was among the first to offer himself. " Let us march immediately," was his proposal, " and never lay down our arms till we obtain our independence." He enlisted as a volunteer, and bade farewell to his school. Before leaving he addressed his pupils most affectionately, gave them earnest counsel, *prayed with them,* and taking each of them by the hand, so bade them farewell.

CHRISTIAN PATRIOTISM.

He wrote to his father, assuring him that a sense of duty prompted him to sacrifice every thing for his country, and promised him that when the war should be over, (and

with his ardent spirit he seems to have had
no doubt of its successful result,) he would
return to his studies, and fit himself for the
sacred profession to which he had been
devoted. Mr. Hale, his father, was a truly
patriotic man. It is said that he would not
allow the wool raised on his farm to be used
in his family, but reserved it to be prepared
and woven into blankets for the army. Also,
it was a habit of his to sit upon his stoop to
watch for the soldiers as they passed his
house, footsore and weary, when he would
call them in and feed and clothe them, and
contribute in any way most needed to their
relief and comfort. Of course such a father
would not refuse to give up his son at the
call of his country.

On the 6th of July, Nathan Hale enlisted
as lieutenant in the 3d company of the 7th
Connecticut regiment, commanded by Colonel Charles Webb. Before he left he
addressed a note to the proprietors of the
school in which he had been engaged, stating
what he had done, and expressing the hope
that as only two weeks of his term of service remained to be fulfilled, they would re-
lease him and suffer him to go at once.
Having an opportunity for "more extended

public service," he says, he feels inclined to go. We hear nothing of the dreams of ambition, nothing of striving for glory ; only an earnest desire to be where he could be of *most use* to the world.

The company to which Hale was attached was ordered first, under the direction of the Council of Safety, to remain for a time for the defense of New London, supposed to be in danger from British ships of war, then off the coast. Regular military duty was performed, and some defenses thrown up ; but on the 14th of September, 1775, in consequence of urgent and imperative orders from the commander-in-chief, all the troops proceeded to join General Washington at Boston. In January, 1776, Hale received a commission as captain in the 19th regiment, and remained in and near Boston until April, when his regiment was ordered to New York.

HIS JOURNAL.

A brief journal kept at this period is preserved, embracing, with some interruptions, the period from September, 1775, to the time of his going to New York. It is principally occupied with records of marches and expeditions, efforts to provide for his men, and notes showing the incessant care and watchfulness which were needed, as the enemy were *so near*. At times he could hear their men at work with their pickaxes, or sometimes in the stillness of the night, the voices of their guard might be heard in their rounds, giving the countersign.

We learn incidentally the fact of the constant observance of daily prayers in the camp. In the intervals of leisure the men did not neglect amusements and athletic sports; games at checkers and games at football are noted, and on one occasion a "wrestling match," the challenge formally given and accepted; and Hale writes in his diary, "Evening prayers omitted for wrestling."

On the Sundays also he refers to the services, seldom omitted except in case of necessity: "Went to meeting in the barn; one exercise. . . . Mr. L. preached, John 13: 19 — excellentissime . . . no meeting in the morning . . . afternoon, Mr. Bird preached."

"Sabbath Day, 19th. — Mr. Bird preached, one service only. Text, Esther 8: 6. 'For how can I endure to see the evil that shall

come upon my people, or how can I endure
to see the destruction of my kindred?' The
discourse very good, the same as preached to
General Wooster, his officers and soldiers, at
New Haven, and which was again preached
at Cambridge a Sabbath or two ago. Now
preached as a farewell discourse."

" 17th, Sunday. — Went to Mistick to
meeting."

Hale was a faithful officer. Indeed, meager
as are the records of his life, we have constant proofs of his stern, strict regard to
duty and right as the rule of his life. He
took great pains to study and learn his duties
as an officer, and to train his raw and rest-
less recruits, writing down from the general
orders directions for the guards, and also
how to practice and drill his men. He induced them to adopt a simple uniform, and
to pay great regard to their own neatness
of appearance, which not only contributed
greatly to their outward improvement, but
led others to follow their example. He
devoted himself to his men, taking care of
their wages, attending to their rations, their
clothing, their comfort in every particular;
and how much an officer may do or may
neglect, only a soldier can know. As a

2

consequence they were much attached to him, and some of his boys assured him that "if their mothers would but consent, they would prefer being with him to all the pleasures which the company of their relatives could afford."

At one time there arose discontent among the men, and their term of service having expired, many of them resolved to return to their homes. They had enlisted for a limited period; some of them were poorly fed, clothed, and paid, and it was with great difficulty that they were persuaded to remain. Hale joined with some of the other officers in offering every inducement to the men to stay; and the following is the entry in his journal, November 28, 1775: —

"Promised the men, if they would tarry for another month, they should have my wages for that time."

This promise he kept, borrowing the money from a brother officer on the credit of the pay due to him.

DEVOTION TO HIS COUNTRY'S CAUSE.

In the new organization of the army, Hale was one of the first to offer himself, and also made every exertion to procure recruits, and to induce men to enlist.

Hale went with his regiment to New York in April, 1776 ; and of his personal movements during that season there is no record. We have only the narrative of one adventure. A British sloop laden with supplies was anchored in the East River, directly under the guns of the enemy's batteries. Captain Hale, with a party of picked men, at the dead hour of the night, with muffled oars, crept over to the other side, seized the sloop, silenced the single watchman who was on deck, and quietly assumed the command. Favored by the darkness they hoisted sail, and quickly moved the sloop over to the other side of the river, when the supplies it contained were gladly received by our own suffering troops, and at once appropriated to their use.

LETTERS.

Two or three letters written to his family at this time are still preserved. In one of them, dated August 20, 1776, he says, " For about six or eight days, the enemy have been expected hourly, whenever the wind and tide in the least favored. We keep a particular lookout for them this morning. The place and manner of attack time must

determine. The event we leave to Heaven.
Thanks to God, we have had time for completing our works and receiving our reënforcements. The militia from Connecticut
ordered this way are mostly arrived. Troops
from the southward are daily coming. We
hope, under God, to give a good account of
the enemy, whenever they choose to make
the last appeal."

Soon after this time was fought the disastrous battle of Long Island, to add new discouragement to our already disheartened
army. They were encamped at various
points, from the Battery for miles up the
Island, while the British army lay on Long
Island, at points directly opposite. The
latter numbered twenty-five thousand men,
were well supplied with provisions, and
equipped with all the necessaries for a long
and successful campaign.

CRITICAL STATE OF AFFAIRS.

The Americans were poorly supplied —
short of provisions, clothing, money, and ammunition, in every way destitute, and only
numbering about fourteen thousand effective
men. The enemy evidently meditated an
attack, but at what point it was impossible

to guess; and with so many miles to defend, so many exposed points, the number of our men was not equal to guarding efficiently every place exposed to attack. Our officers were ignorant of the number and disposition of the enemy, who was every day growing stronger, while our forces were becoming weaker and more discouraged.

Should their troops cross at any intermediate point, they might divide our already weakened army, and hem in a portion in the lower part of the Island, cut off from means of escape. Or, if our troops retreated to the northward, the whole lower portion of the Island would be in their power.

In these circumstances, Washington earnestly desired that some one should be found who could penetrate the enemy's lines, and gain such information as would enable him to prepare to meet them on terms more nearly equal. A mere common soldier, as a spy, would not answer his purpose, as he needed reports of the plans of the camps, the military disposition of the troops, and, if possible, some idea of their intentions, while the messenger would require peculiar wisdom and tact in evading inquiry, and passing unsuspected and unharmed through a hostile camp.

Washington communicated his wishes to Colonel Knowlton, that they might be made known, and diligent inquiry be made for any one who would be willing to undertake so dangerous an errand. But it was not easy at once to find any one to volunteer for work like that proposed. The business of a spy involves more danger than either honor or profit. The reward is not proportioned to the risk of certain death in case of detection.

Application was made to a French sergeant, who had served in the French war, with the hope that he would not be as scrupulous, and that his daring spirit of adventure, which had led him to cross the ocean to fight with us, might prompt him to undertake the expedition. "No, no," he answered promptly, "I am ready to fight the British at any place and time, but I do not feel willing to go among them to be hung up like a dog."

HALE VOLUNTEERS AS A SPY.

The case looked desperate, and Colonel Knowlton was preparing to report to General

Washington that none could be found ready
for so dangerous an errand, when, in the
silence of the disappointed assemblage of
officers, arose a clear voice, saying, "I will
undertake it." It was the voice of Captain
Nathan Hale. Who shall tell what a struggle had passed in his mind; what waves of
doubt and uncertainty had rolled over him;
what a giving up of cherished hopes and
sundering of the nearest ties; what upward,
earnest prayer for strength, before he could
come to the resolution thus to risk all?

His friends, his military friends, remon-
strated with him upon the sacrifice he proposed — the risk he incurred. If he were
successful, he gained little honor; if he
failed, there was no result but *death*, sudden
and disgraceful. "He spoke," said Hull,
" with warmth and decision, and this was his
answer:

" ' I think I owe to my country the accomplishment of an object so important, and so
much desired by the commander of her
armies — and I know no other mode of
obtaining the information than by assuming
a disguise and passing into the enemy's
camp. I .am fully sensible of the conse-
quences of discovery and capture in such a

situation. *But for a year I have been attached
to the army, and have not rendered any mate-
rial service, while receiving a compensation
for which I make no return.*

" 'Yet I am not influenced by the expecta-
tion of promotion or pecuniary reward. *I
wish to be useful, and every kind of service
necessary for the public good becomes honorable by being necessary.* If the exigencies
of my country demand a peculiar service,
its claims to the performance of that service
are imperious.'" And so he prepared himself for the undertaking.

Hale was absent about two weeks. He
went up from Harlem to Norwalk, with his
faithful attendant Asher Wright, left with
him his uniform and all his effects except
his diploma, adopted the plain brown dress
and broad-brimmed hat of the schoolmaster,
and departed on his perilous errand. He
crossed in a vessel to Long Island, and was
set on shore from a small boat, near Huntington, making arrangements for the boat
to meet him at a given time and place, in
obedience to certain signals. From that
time nothing is known of his movements.
During his absence a part of the British
army had crossed the river to New York,

and occupied the city for two miles above
the Battery, while another force was stretched
across the Island, about seven miles higher
up. The American troops were encamped
above this point.

HIS DETECTION AND CAPTURE.

Hale, in his wanderings, must have pene-
trated their lines, made himself familiar
with their camps, their numbers and strength.
In the completeness of his disguise, he may,
in his intercourse with them, have learned
something of their plans and intentions —
must have crossed to New York and re-
crossed to Long Island. He had passed
safely through all these dangers, and was on
his return already on the shore where he
had disembarked. Still in his character of
schoolmaster, he had stopped at a house,
met several persons, and partaken of some
refreshment. Standing on the shore, await-
ing the boat which was to come in obedience
to his signal, he went forward as a boat ap-
proached, and when it was too late, perceived
his mistake. It was a British boat, and the
muskets of the soldiers were leveled at
him. He attempted to retreat, but it was
too late; any movement to escape was certain

death — so he resigned himself to his fate.
Various stories are told as to the manner of
his betrayal. By some it was asserted that
it was by a renegade countryman, who had
formerly known him, and who recognized
him at the last place at which he stopped.
Let us hope that no American was vile
enough for such a service.

Be that as it may, from a British vessel
which lay around the point, out of sight, a
boat had been sent for his capture, and the
attempt was but too successful. He was put
on board the vessel, and speedily conveyed
to New York. He had been previously
searched. The very fact of his being there,
within the enemy's lines, *an officer of the
American army*, was proof against him. As
a truthful man he could give no other account of himself. In the search nothing
was found upon him but his college diploma,
which had perhaps aided him in maintaining
his disguise; but, on further examination,
there were found, under the inner soles of his
shoes, thin pieces of paper, on which were
drawn accurate plans of the enemy's camps,
with notes in Latin which could bear but
one interpretation. It would be vain to
attempt to deny the fact. *He was a Spy.*

HIS CONVICTION AND EXECUTION.

Immediately on arriving in New York, Hale was brought before General Howe, whose head quarters were in that city. The house is said to be still standing, about three and a quarter miles from the Park, and now at the corner of Fifty-first Street and First Avenue, the property of the Beekman family. In the same house, André, the British spy, spent his last night in New York, before going up the river on his ill-fated expedition. Hale's arrival was on the 21st day of September, a day marked as the date of a fearful conflagration which swept over a large portion of the city.

Hale appeared before General Howe. The charges were made; the proof was clear; there could be no question, no explanation, no evasion. He did not attempt to deny his position, and only regretted that his efforts, thus far successful, had been suddenly arrested, and that he had done no good. The trial was short, the sentence summary — that he should be removed to prison, and hanged "to-morrow morning at daybreak." The prison in which he spent his few remaining hours is said to be the old prison, in one of the buildings still standing at the north end of the City Hall Park. Here he was committed to the tender mercies of the Provost Marshal Cunningham, a brutal and unfeeling wretch, proverbial for his cruelties.

Here, with but a few hours between him and death, Nathan Hale spent that dismal night. He was denied the privilege of seeing a clergyman — a favor seldom refused to the vilest felons; was not allowed a Bible, or even pens and paper for a last communication to his absent friends. Finally, at the urgent solicitation of a young lieutenant, who was interested in his fate and moved by the sudden and violent manner in which it had overtaken him, the last indulgence was granted.

Alas, that words so precious should have been lost to his heart-broken friends and to his countrymen! But when his letters were written, they were examined, of course, by his brutal jailer, who grew furiously angry at the noble sentiments expressed in them, and at once destroyed every line. He gave his own reasons afterward — " *The rebels should never know they had a man who could die with so much firmness.*"

This is all we know of the events of that fearful night, the last hours of a young and brave spirit cut off in the midst of his days, when life had so much of brightness and hope in its future. Hale was a Christian man; his refuge was in God, and we can not doubt he was sustained in that hour of bitter trial, with no earthly friend near—not even a minister of religion—to receive a message or speak words of peace to his sinking soul.

Hale was executed at daybreak, according to his sentence; and the only particulars that could be learned were such as could be gathered long afterward from such strangers as chanced to be present, spectators of the scene. A file of soldiers was marched out, and Hale was conducted to the place of execution, and ·hanged on a tree, his execution being marked by the same brutality which had added bitterness to his last hours, destroyed the last records of his life, the letters which would have given some comfort to the friends who could never cease to mourn his sad fate. The place of his execution and the place of his burial are equally unknown, though both were said to have been in the neighborhood of his prison.

His memory passed away, save from the heart-broken friends who mourned for him. His mother never recovered from the blow.

The memory of Nathan Hale was unhonored, and while André's name was on every tongue, while the English nation gave him a place in Westminster Abbey and erected a monument to his memory, and even our own countrymen spoke with sympathy of his untimely fate, the name of Hale, the martyr, is hardly known.

A few years since, by a great effort, funds were raised in his native town, to which the State of Connecticut contributed, and a granite monument was erected to his memory. On it are recorded the last words of the patriot — the martyr : —

"I only regret that I have but one life to lose for my country."

SORROW IN THE AMERICAN ARMY AT HIS DEATH.

The capture and execution of Hale were considered of sufficient importance to be communicated formally by the British to the American General. He was mourned as a brother by the other officers who had known, esteemed, loved him, and by none more sincerely regretted than by Washington himself. At his request Hale had gone on his perilous expedition. He had esteemed him as a faithful and zealous officer, one of those whom his country could trust, and from whom it had much to hope.

Only his dying words were permitted to reach them, by way of consolation; but they showed the power which sustained the patriot martyr even in his last hour, and in the bitter agony of such a death.

André also spoke dying words, but they were of himself: "I pray you to bear me witness that I meet my fate like a brave man!" In Hale spoke the patriot — "I only regret that I have but one life to lose for my country."

Noble words, showing the spirit which actuated the man; patriotism sustained and upheld by religion. He would go where he could be most useful to his country; he would do that service which his country most needed; not that which would bring most fame or glory to himself. He would risk life, and the loss of all that made life dear, for this beloved land.

Nathan Hale was ready to die, for he was a Christian — a Christian soldier. He was a man of prayer. He prayed with his scholars when he took leave of them, — as it proved to meet them no more; he prayed for his men, and his labor and his prayers went together. The habitual desire and fixed determination *to do right* seldom left him in doubt as to the course he should pursue. It made him a dutiful and affectionate son, a faithful teacher, an earnest, conscientious officer, a devoted patriot, an efficient spy — a good soldier of Jesus Christ, to whose service as a minister he proposed to devote himself, and sustained him at the last moment of bitter trial. Then, we believe, he was not alone, for his Saviour was with him, saying, " Be thou faithful unto death, and I will give thee a crown of life." So ended his life, on that bright Sabbath morning, the last he should see on earth.

We mourn over the loss of the last records of his life, traced by his own hand, on that fearful night when, in the full tide of youthful health, and strength, and hope, he was to be cut down suddenly — when "daybreak" was the signal to cut him off from life. But from what we know of the man, and even from the admissions of his brutal jailer, we can not doubt they breathed the same spirit which spoke forth in those words, uttered in his last moments :

" I only regret that I have but one life to lose for my country."

MEN WANTED.

Passing down the street a few days since, we were attracted by a large placard, on which were printed in mammoth capitals the significant words, " *Men Wanted!*" and as we continued our way and saw the crowds that hurried past us, the capitals frequently flashed in our eyes, "Men Wanted!"

Yes! we thought to ourselves, *Men* are wanted! Not things of straw in the shape of men, that have no substance or reality about them ; mere bundles of nothings, tied up with a tailor's band, in the extreme of the fashionable cut, to keep them from being blown away ; brainless, and careless of life and its duties—who think of none but themselves and their vanity, and who act as if life were a jest, a bubble, and a dream.

Men wanted! Not a fop who will sit before a photographer's lens to be reduced to his true size in the world, and to have his true value rated on the back of his shadow in the price of the revenue-stamp gummed on the card. Such characters are not sought after in the present case.

Men wanted! Not the sordid wretch who will grasp the last farthing from the hands of the suffering widow or the helpless orphan, to swell his gains. Not the hoarder of wealth gotten by the oppression of the poor, and the extortion and raud practiced upon the rich. Not the calculating grasp-all who will do only what he thinks will be for his own advantage, and forgets that his interests are united with those around him. Such are not wanted.

Men wanted! Not cowards, who shiver and slink away in the face of duty, and are ready to betray themselves and their cause at the least difficulty; whose hearts sink within them at the demands of real and earnest effort, and who fall to the rear in the hour of struggle! Such are not wanted.

Men wanted! Not bounty-jumpers, who enlist that they may pocket the bounty and then fly from the service they have engaged to perform, like those who receive large blessings from the hand of Providence, and think they can escape rendering their service and their account—mere bounty-jumpers of God's goodness, who will find that there is a reserve corps from which they can not escape.

None of these. But MEN are wanted in the great struggle of the Republic for Freedom, Righteousness and Temperance. The brave soul and the loyal heart, that can feel and understand the value of the blessings at stake, for to-day and for all time, not only for our own country, but for the world.

MEN WANTED—with earnest soul and iron will to go out into the great work of the age, and do battle for the truth against oppression and wrong in all their forms. Men whose thoughts are blazing truths, and whose words are trumpet-peals to action and to duty—who can not rest except when they bear the armor, and can not sleep except on the well-won battle-field!

MEN WANTED—to carry the banner of peace and progress, of freedom and righteousness, high aloft over the corruptions and follies of the world ; who, trampling its bribes and its allurements under their feet, will stop only when it is planted high on the glory-crowned battlements of the future. Men of faith and hope—men of truth and love—men of mind and will— men of power and nerve—men of clear sight and clean hearts—men who stoop low down to the humblest children of earth that they may raise them to be the children of heaven—such MEN are WANTED in the ranks to-day!

www.ingramcontent.com/pod-product-compliance
Lightning Source LLC
Chambersburg PA
CBHW021452090426
42739CB00009B/1731